WAYS INTO GEOGRAPHY

A Visit to the Seaside

Louise Spilsbury

W

FRANKLIN WATTS
LONDON·SYDNEY

First published in 2009 by
Franklin Watts
338 Euston Road
London NW1 3BH

Franklin Watts Australia
Level 17/207 Kent Street
Sydney NSW 2000

Copyright © Franklin Watts 2009

Series editor: Julia Bird
Art director: Jonathan Hair
Design: Shobha Mucha
Consultant: Sam Woodhouse, Associate Consultant for
Geography & Citizenship, Somerset

A CIP catalogue record for this book is available
from the British Library.

Picture credits:
Alamy: 12: (t) © Skyscan Photolibrary; 14: (t) © Jack Sullivan; 16: (t) © Nick &
Suzanne Geary; (b) © Alan Curtis; 19: (t) © D Burke; (b) John Periam/Sylvia Cordaiy
Photo Library Ltd; 22: © Jack Sullivan; 24: © The Photolibrary Wales; 27: © Steffan
Hill. Corbis: © MedioImages. Istockphoto.com: 7: (m) © istockphoto; 8: (b) Rene
Mansi; 10: (m) © Charlie Bishop; 11: (t) Ferran Traite Soler; (b) Gordon Dixon; 12: (b)
© Stephen Rees; 17: (b) Eliza Snow; 18: (t) © istockphoto; 20: (t) © Martin Bowker;
(m) Andrew Howe; (b) Mary Marin; 22: (t) © Silke Dietze; 25: (br) Matt Stauss.
Science Photo Library: (l & r) © Andrew J Martinez. Shutterstock: cover: (l) Jacqueline
Abromelt; (r) Peter Guess; 7: (t) TTphoto; (b): © David Hughes; 8: (t) Ana de Sousa; 9:
(t) Stephen Aaron Rees; (b) Eric Gevaert; 10 (t) © Jacqueline Abromeit; (b): © Martin
Horsky; 11: (m) © Shutterstock; 14: (b) © Shutterstock; 17: (t) © ronfrom york; 18: (b)
© Kevin Britland; 23: (t) © Kuzma; (b) MdN; 25: (t) © Susannah Grant; 26: (tl) ©
Amber Shock; (tr) Margo Harrison; (ml) © nicobatista; (mr) Cheryl Casey; (bl): ©
Ronen; 27: (b) © shaileshnanal.

Every attempt has been made to clear copyright.
Should there be any inadvertent omission, please apply to
the publisher for rectification.

ISBN 978 0 7496 8733 5
Dewey Classification: 394.269

Printed in China

Franklin Watts is a division of Hachette Children's Books,
an Hachette UK company.
www.hachette.co.uk

Contents

Beside the sea

The seaside is the place where land and sea meet.

The land by the edge of the sea is called the shore or beach. It is always changing because of the movement of the tides.

At high tide, the beach is covered with water.

At low tide, the sea has gone out.

The seaside is one kind of environment or place. What other types of place can you think of?

△ City

△ Village

▽ Countryside

Which type of environment do you live in?

Which would you like to visit? Why?

Sorting seasides

There are different kinds of seasides.

Some seasides have steep cliffs.

Rocky beaches may have rock pools when the tide goes out.

This seaside is covered in soft sand.

Dunes are hills of sand. Many seaside dunes are covered in long grass.

Seaside buildings

Some buildings are special to seaside towns.

Piers are for fun. They allow people to walk over the water.

Harbour walls protect a seaside town from the force of the waves.

Do you know what this is? What is it for?

Seaside shops sell things you need or find at the seaside. What do these seaside shops sell?

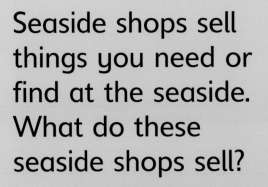

What do the shops in your local area sell?

FISH & CHIPS

My town, your town

Maya compares photos of her town and a seaside town.

What is the same? What is different?

Maya makes a list of some of the differences between her town and a seaside town.

Seaside	My town
Lighthouse	No lighthouse
Harbour wall	No harbour wall
Beach to play on	Castle to visit
Sea nearby	Hills nearby
Seaside shops	Shopping centre

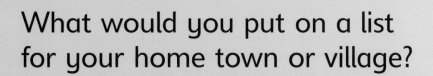

What would you put on a list for your home town or village?

Like and dislike

Why do people visit the seaside? What do they do there?

Sam likes going on donkey rides.

Amy likes to build sandcastles at the beach.

What would you like to do at the seaside?

Amy's class makes a pictogram of the things they like to do at the seaside.

	Paddling	Eating ice cream	Seaside rides	Building sandcastles	Sunbathing
1			🐴	🏰	
2			🐴	🏰	
3			🐴	🏰	
4			🐴	🏰	
5			🐴	🏰	
6			🐴	🏰	
7			🐴	🏰	
8			🐴		
9			🐴		

No one likes sunbathing!
Which is the favourite activity?
What jobs do people who live at the seaside do? Turn the page to find out.

Seaside people

Some people at the seaside look after tourists.

This lady runs a seaside hotel. She makes beds and cleans rooms for visitors to stay in.

People working at this seaside café make and serve food to tourists.

Fishermen catch fish for people to eat and take visitors out on fishing trips.

This man's job is to teach people how to windsurf.

Who keeps us safe at the seaside? Turn the page to find out.

Seaside Safety

Lifeguards make sure that people are safe when they swim or surf at the seaside.

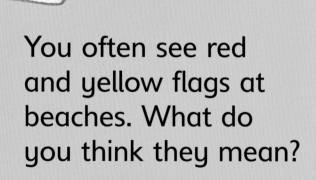

You often see red and yellow flags at beaches. What do you think they mean?

The UK coastguard has boats to help people in trouble at sea.

Sometimes, the coastguard uses helicopters to airlift people to safety.

What jobs do people do in your local area?

Explore the shore

What wildlife can you see at the seaside?

Limpets live on rocks that get covered by the sea when the tide comes in.

Sea birds hover above the sea, looking for small fish to eat.

Crabs often burrow under the sand or hide among seaweed.

Can you see the crab in this picture?

Amy's class made a chart to record the animals they saw on a class trip to the seaside.

Limpets ✓✓✓✓✓✓✓✓ 12

Seagulls ✓✓✓✓✓ 6

 Crabs ✓✓✓ 3

Anemones ✓✓ 2

Starfish 0

Which animal did they see the most? Why do you think that is?

aring for the seaside

Sometimes visitors leave litter at the seaside. Litter includes things like empty plastic bottles and crisp packets.

Litter spoils the seaside because it looks ugly.

Litter can also harm animals. They may get stuck in old bottles or bags, or can mistake litter for food.

People may drop litter if rubbish bins are full, or if the bins are a long way away.

They should take their litter home with them instead.

People could also bring their food in boxes that can be used again, like these.

How else can we reduce the litter at the seaside?

Seaside seasons

Most people visit the seaside in summer when it is warm and sunny.

In winter there can be storms and strong winds at the seaside.

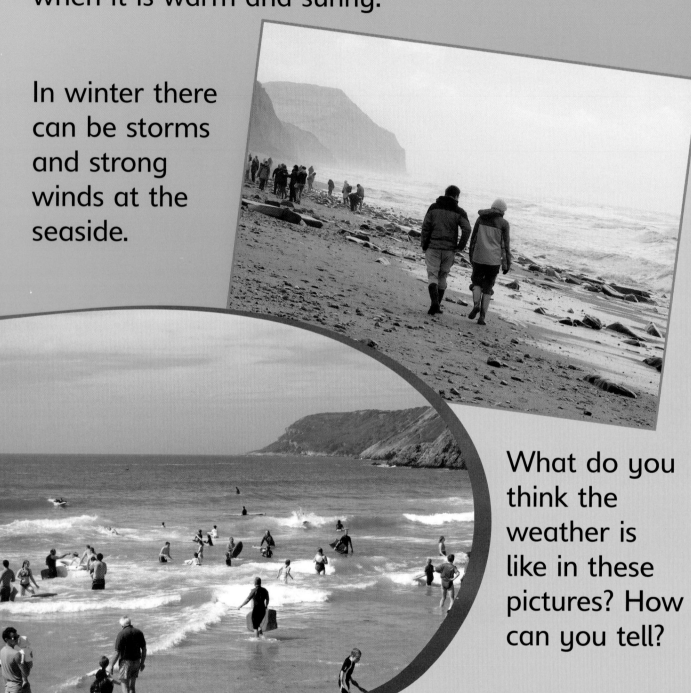

What do you think the weather is like in these pictures? How can you tell?

We wear different clothes in summer and winter.

Welly boots

Straw hat

Scarf

Flip flops

Shorts

Woolly hat

Which of these clothes would you take to the seaside in summer? Which would you take in winter?

Seaside of the World

Where in the world can you have a seaside holiday?

Many people go to hot countries far away for seaside holidays now. To get there, they usually travel by plane or ferry.

Have you ever visited a seaside in another country?

In Australia, Christmas comes during the summer so people head to the beach!

This seaside in India is used by fishermen and tourists.

How are these seaside places different to ones in the UK?

Useful words

Coastguard – a person who works at the seaside. Coastguards check ships and boats are safe and make sure people obey the law at sea, for example by going at the correct speed.

Environment – the area or surroundings in which people or animals live. You might live in a city or seaside environment for example.

Harbour – an area protected from the open sea by land or walls. People use harbours to come to land safely or leave ships safely.

Lifeguard – a person trained in life-saving and water safety. Some lifeguards work at the seaside to keep people safe.

Lighthouse – a tower with lights at the top that shine at night. The lights warn ships of dangerous rocks.

Litter – waste or rubbish that is left out in public places instead of being put into a bin.

Pictogram – a chart or graph that uses pictures or symbols to show and compare information.

Pier – a walkway built out from the shore and over the sea.

Tide – the way the water rises up and then comes back down a beach. High tide is when the sea is highest up a beach. Low tide is when the sea is furthest down a beach.

Tourist – someone who visits a place on holiday.

Some answers

Here are some answers to the questions we have asked in this book. Don't worry if you had different answers to ours; you may be right, too. Talk through your answers with other people and see if you can explain why they are right.

Page 10: The building is a lighthouse. A lighthouse is a tower with lights at the top that shine at night. The lights warn ships of dangerous rocks which the ships might crash into.

Page 11: The shop at the top of the page sells things to use at the seaside, such as inflatable boats, sunglasses and buckets and spades. The shop in the middle of the page sells shells, and the shop at the bottom sells fish and chips.

Page 12: Both towns would be attractive to tourists as they have places, such as the castle and the beach, to visit. They both also have homes and shops. The main difference between the two towns is the environment. Maya's town is surrounded by the countryside, while the seaside town is by the coast.

Page 15: The favourite activity is going on seaside rides.

Page 18: On beaches with lifeguards, it is safe to swim where there is a red and yellow flag showing. This is the area where the lifeguard can see you.

Page 21: The tally chart shows that Amy saw more limpets than any other animal at the seaside. This is partly because limpets sit on the surface of rocks where we can see them.

Page 23: We could reduce litter at the seaside by having more litter bins around, especially at beaches where people sit or by shops where they buy food. Posters telling people about the problems and dangers of litter would also encourage them to dispose of their litter more carefully.

Page 24: We can tell the weather is cold and wintry in the top picture because the sky is grey, the sea is rough, and people are wearing warm clothes. In the bottom picture, we can tell it is warm because the sky is blue and people are swimming in the sea.

Page 25: You would take the straw hat, shorts and flip flops to the beach in summer. You would take the woolly hat, scarf and welly boots to the beach in winter.

Page 27: The seaside in Australia is different because in Australia it is summer when it is winter in the UK. The Indian seaside is different because this is a working village where fishermen and their families live, as well as a place that tourists visit. At seaside resorts in the UK most people work in tourism. At large ports, people work at docks unloading and loading ships and in some seaside towns, people still work in the fishing industry.

Index

About this book

Ways into Geography is designed to encourage children to think about the local and wider world in a geographical way. This title, **A Visit to the Seaside**, is a way in for children to study a contrasting area (assuming that they don't live at the seaside). This is one of the two locality studies required at KS1. By working through this book they will also be learning the following **geographical skills:**
1. How to ask geographical questions (National Curriculum 1a).
2. To use geographical vocabulary (National Curriculum 2a).

Learning content
1. Working with the list (p.13), the pictogram (p.15) and the chart (p.21) helps children 'to observe and record' (National Curriculum 1b).
2. Questions such as 'Which type of environment do you live in? Which would you like to visit? Why?' (p.7) encourage children to 'express their own views about places' (National Curriculum 1c), 'to identify and describe what places are like' (National Curriculum 3a) and 'recognise how places compare with other places' (NC 3d).

Resources and extension activities
To extend the theme of transport, children could investigate how people get to different seaside places in the UK and mark seaside places that the children in the class have visited on a map. To extend the topic of seasides around the world explored on pages 26–7, you could give groups a set of overseas travel brochures to identify between a number of seaside places around the world and find them on a map. They could also explain to others which of those places they would like to visit and why. Finally, aerial photographs of seaside places could be compared with simple maps of the same area to introduce basic map vocabulary.